I0796611

May 21 – June 21

Christine Webster

www.av2books.com

**Step 1**
Go to **www.av2books.com**

**Step 2**
Enter this unique code
**VMERBRZ2M**

**Step 3**
Explore your interactive eBook!

**AV2 is optimized for use on any device**

# Your interactive eBook comes with...

**Contents**
Browse a live contents page to easily navigate through resources

**Audio**
Listen to sections of the book read aloud

**Videos**
Watch informative video clips

**Weblinks**
Gain additional information for research

**Try This!**
Complete activities and hands-on experiments

**Key Words**
Study vocabulary, and complete a matching word activity

**Quizzes**
Test your knowledge

**Slideshows**
View images and captions

**... and much, much more!**

# GEMINI

May 21 – June 21

## Contents

# Are You a Gemini?

Do you learn quickly? Are you considered to be a kind person? If this describes you, you might be a Gemini. A Gemini is someone who was born between May 21 and June 21.

Gemini is a sign in the zodiac. This is a series of 12 **constellations** that run across the night sky. For centuries, people have used these groups of stars to tell the future. The study of the stars in this manner is called astrology.

# Zodiac Chart

**A person's zodiac sign is determined by his or her date of birth. Which sign matches your birthday?**

# It's in the Stars

The zodiac constellations form a circle around Earth. In one year, Earth makes a full **orbit** around the Sun. As it does this, the Sun appears to be in different places at set times. The zodiac constellations are found along the path the Sun follows.

Long ago, people used the Sun to tell the time of year. In late May, the Sun passed through the Gemini constellation. People born then were said to be born under the sign of Gemini.

Over time, the position of the constellations shifted. Even though the Sun now passes through Gemini at a different time, the dates associated with the sign of Gemini remain the same.

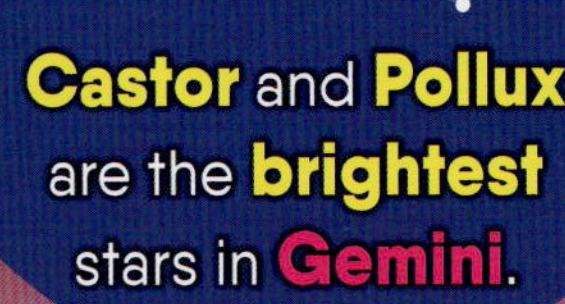


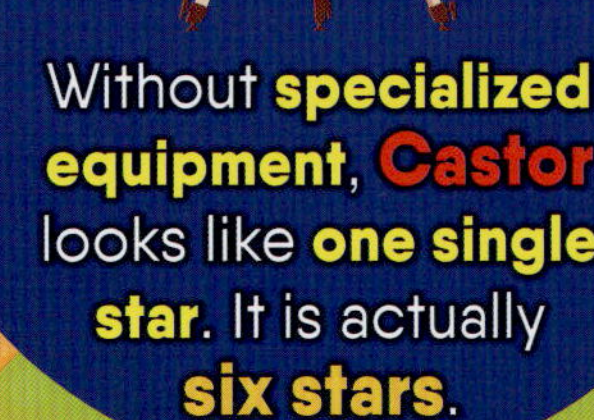

Castor and Pollux are known as the twins.

# The Myth of Gemini

The ancient Greeks had stories about how each zodiac constellation came to be in the sky. Gemini is linked to a pair of twins named Castor and Pollux.

The boys had the same mother, the queen of Sparta, but different fathers. Castor's father was the king of Sparta. Pollux's father was the Greek god Zeus. This made Castor a human and Pollux a **demigod**.

As a demigod, Pollux was **immortal**, but Castor was not. Even so, they loved going on daring adventures together. On one such adventure, Castor was killed.

Pollux was devastated by Castor's death. He begged his father to allow him to share his immortality, so he and Castor could be together forever. Zeus put Castor and Pollux in the sky as stars in the constellation Gemini. The pair can both still be seen there today.

Together, Castor and Pollux are known as the *Dioscuri* in Greek.

# Gemini and Mutable Signs

In astrology, some zodiac signs share certain **qualities**. These qualities show how a person acts in the world. The qualities are separated into three groups. Cardinal signs are known for inspiring a plan. Fixed signs help to complete the plan. Mutable signs make sure the plan is perfected.

Gemini is a mutable sign. People in this group understand that good things must sometimes come to an end. They use their experiences to prepare for such circumstances. Mutable signs help others adapt to different situations as well.

Mutable signs can sometimes seem older and wiser than their years.

# Zodiac Signs
## by Quality

### Cardinal Signs
Are known for inspiring a plan.

Aries

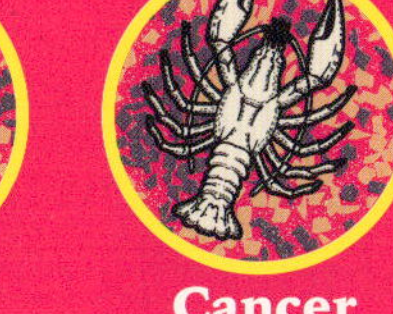
Cancer

Libra

Capricorn

### Fixed Signs
Help to complete the plan.

Taurus

Leo

Scorpio

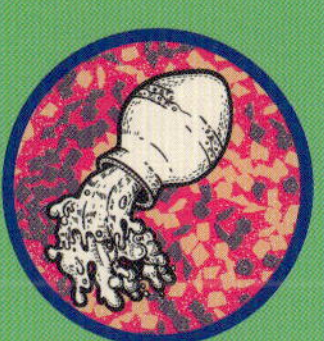
Aquarius

### Mutable Signs
Make sure the plan is perfected.

Gemini

Virgo

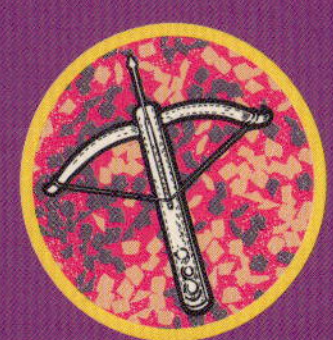
Sagittarius

Pisces

# Gemini as an Air Sign

Zodiac signs are also grouped according to the four **classical elements**. These are fire, earth, water, and air. Signs that belong to the same group share common personality traits.

Gemini is an air sign. Air people are good at expressing how they feel. They typically enjoy **socializing** with others. Air signs are very good communicators. They also love to analyze things.

✷ If you have a problem, seek help from an air sign. They tend to be rational and think things through carefully.

# Zodiac Signs
## by Element

Fire

Aries

Leo

Sagittarius

Earth

Taurus

Virgo

Capricorn

Air

Gemini

Libra

Aquarius

Water

Cancer

Scorpio

Pisces

# Being a Gemini

A Gemini's air traits and mutable qualities combine to create a specific type of person. A key Gemini strength is having a thirst for knowledge. Geminis are very **curious**. They love to learn and often have a book in their hands.

Geminis have their weaknesses as well. Their quest for so much information can sometimes cause them to be unfocused. Geminis also like to have a good time. Due to this, they may not take certain situations very seriously.

**Gemini is ruled by the planet Mercury.** This is the planet of **knowledge** and **technology.**

**Mercury** is **3,032 miles** in diameter. (4,880 kilometers)

Geminis are good at team sports because of their willingness to work with all team members.

# Geminis through Time

Geminis have had a significant impact on the world over time. They have led nations, set records, and won awards. Their contributions have helped make the world what it is today.

English royal **George V** (born June 3, 1865) becomes king of the United Kingdom, and rules until his death in 1936.

Actress **Marilyn Monroe** (born June 1, 1926) stars in the film *Some Like It Hot*, and wins a Golden Globe Award for her performance the following year.

**1960**

Politician **John F. Kennedy** (born May 29, 1917) becomes the youngest person ever elected as president of the United States, at age 43.

**1991**

Supermodel **Naomi Campbell** (born May 22, 1970) becomes the first black model to appear on the cover of *Time* magazine.

**2011**

English royal **Prince William** (born June 21, 1982) marries Kate Middleton at Westminster Abbey in London, England.

**2020**

Professional tennis player **Novak Djokovic** (born May 22, 1987) is ranked the #1 men's singles tennis player in the world.

# Making Friends

Some people believe that zodiac signs can help people form relationships. Each sign has its own traits. These traits can be a good fit with other signs. A Gemini might know ahead of time if someone will be a good friend just by finding out his or her sign.

## It's Friendship

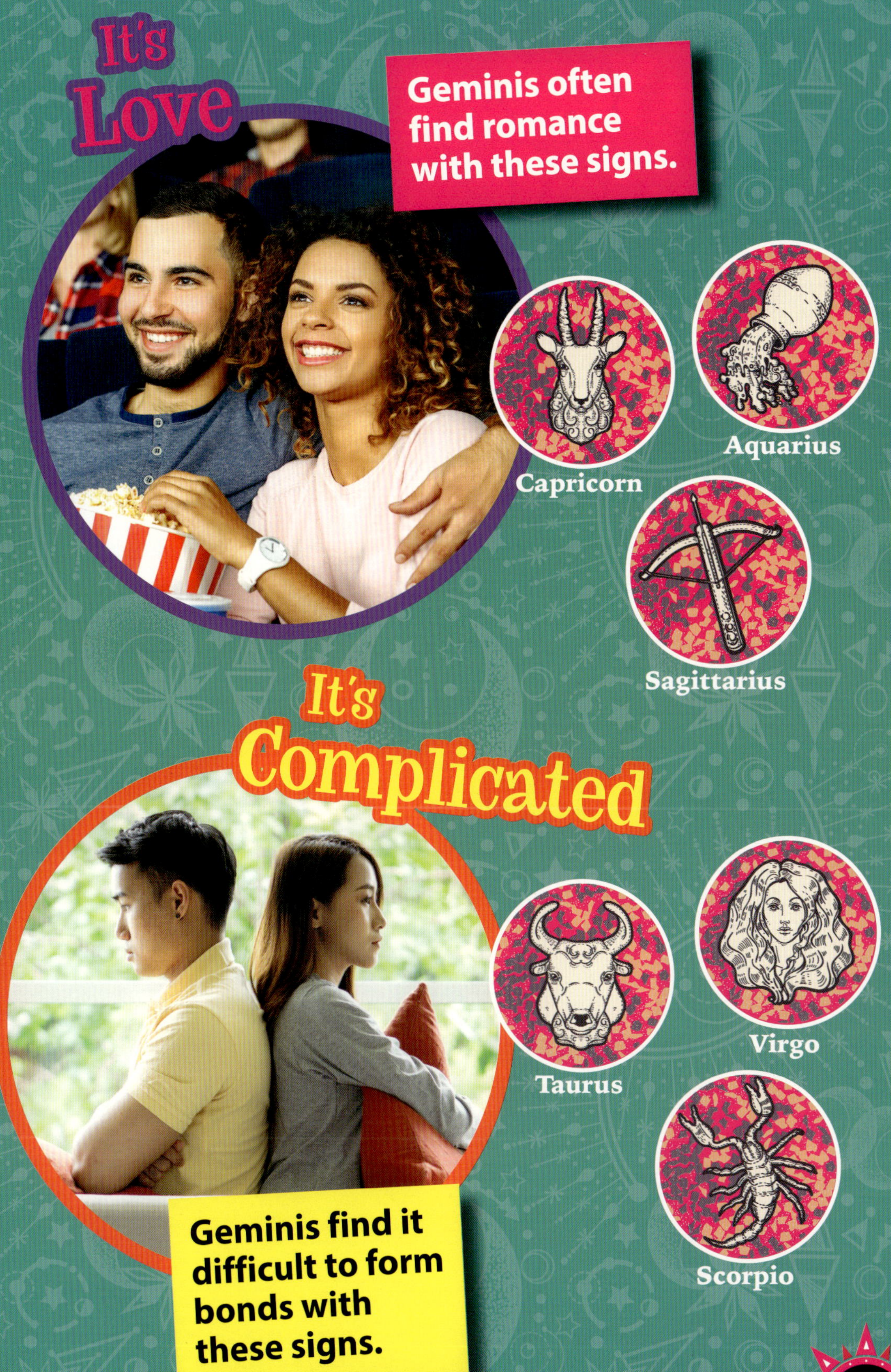
It's Love
Geminis often find romance with these signs.
Capricorn
Aquarius
Sagittarius
It's Complicated
Taurus
Virgo
Scorpio
Geminis find it difficult to form bonds with these signs.

# Know Your Geminis

Geminis continue to make an impact on the world. They can be found doing good work in various fields. Did you know these people are Geminis?

## Angelina Jolie

**Born:** June 4, 1975

Angelina Jolie played famed Disney villain Maleficent in the 2014 film of the same name. She is set to become part of the popular **Marvel Cinematic Universe (MCU)** in 2021, as Thena in *The Eternals*. Angelina is also a **humanitarian**. She spent more than a decade as a **Goodwill Ambassador** for the United Nations (UN). Since 2012, she has served the UN in an expanded role, as a Special Envoy.

Angelina reprised her role as Maleficent in 2019's *Maleficent: Mistress of Evil.*

## Macklemore

**Born:** June 19, 1983

Ben Haggerty is better known by his stage name, Macklemore. Along with collaborator Ryan Lewis, the rapper won four Grammy Awards in 2014. He also has his own YouTube channel. On it, the single "Thrift Shop" has more than 1.4 billion views to date.

## Aly Raisman

**Born:** May 25, 1994

Aly Raisman started taking gymnastics classes when she was only 2 years old. She found fame as a member of the 2012 U.S. Olympic women's gymnastics team, the "Fierce Five." Aly took home three medals, making her the most-decorated U.S. gymnast that year. She won another three Olympic medals in 2016.

## Chris Pratt

**Born:** June 21, 1979

Actor Chris Pratt first rose to fame on the sitcom *Parks and Recreation*. He has since gone on to have a successful movie career. Chris joined the MCU as Peter Quill in the 2014 film, *Guardians of the Galaxy*, a role he has reprised multiple times. Chris also stars in the popular *Jurassic World* **franchise**.

## Venus Williams

**Born:** June 17, 1980

Venus Williams is one of the world's best professional tennis players. Over her career, she has won four Olympic gold medals. Along with her sister Serena, she has won 22 doubles titles. Venus also holds an impressive 49 singles titles.

# The Gemini QUIZ

**1**

Who was the twin of Pollux?

**2**

How many zodiac constellations are there?

**3**

Astrology is the study of what?

**4**

With which signs do Geminis find it difficult to form bonds?

**6**

What planet rules Gemini?

**5**

Is a Gemini a cardinal, fixed, or mutable sign?

**7**

Which celebrity Gemini is a humanitarian and an actress?

**8**

To which element group do Geminis belong?

ANSWERS: 1. Castor 2. 12 3. The study of stars to tell the future
4. Taurus, Virgo, and Scorpio 5. Mutable 6. Mercury 7. Angelina Jolie 8. Air

# Key Words

**classical elements:** materials from which all other materials were once believed to be made

**constellations:** groups of stars that form patterns in the sky

**curious:** a desire to find things out

**demigod:** the offspring of a human and a god

**franchise:** a collection of related films

**Goodwill Ambassador:** someone who advocates for a global issue or cause, as a notable public figure

**humanitarian:** someone who is concerned with the welfare of others

**immortal:** able to live forever

**Marvel Cinematic Universe (MCU):** a series of superhero films, based on characters that appear in Marvel comic books

**orbit:** a regular, repeating path that one object in space takes around another

**qualities:** traits that make something what it is

**socializing:** going out or meeting with friends

# Index

# Get the best of both worlds.

AV2 bridges the gap between print and digital.

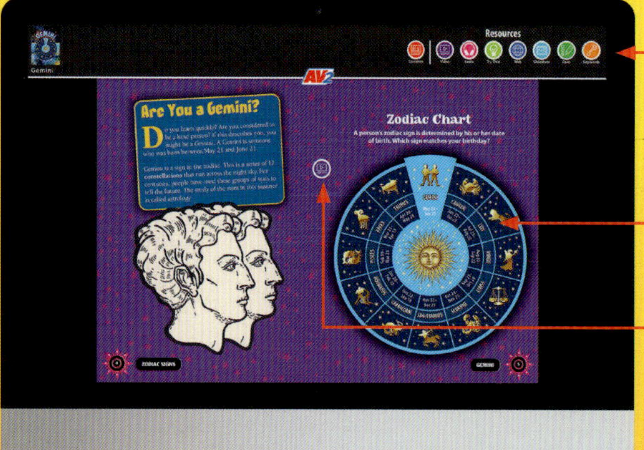


The expandable resources toolbar enables quick access to content including **videos**, **audio**, **activities**, **weblinks**, **slideshows**, **quizzes**, and **key words**.

**Animated videos** make static images come alive.

Resource icons on each page help readers to further **explore key concepts**.

Published by AV2
14 Penn Plaza 9th Floor
New York, NY 10122
Website: www.av2books.com



Library of Congress Control Number: 2020938550

ISBN 978-1-7911-2624-7 (hardcover)
ISBN 978-1-7911-2625-4 (softcover)
ISBN 978-1-7911-2626-1 (multi-user eBook)
ISBN 978-1-7911-2627-8 (single-user eBook)

Printed in Guangzhou, China
1 2 3 4 5 6 7 8 9 0 24 23 22 21 20

062020
101119

Editor: Katie Gillespie
Art Director: Terry Paulhus

Every reasonable effort has been made to trace ownership and to obtain permission to reprint copyright material. The publisher would be pleased to have any errors or omissions brought to their attention so that they may be corrected in subsequent printings.

AV2 acknowledges Getty Images, Alamy, iStock, and Shutterstock as its primary image suppliers for this title.